The Space Between: Identifying Cultural Canyons in Online Spaces and the use of LatinX Culture to Bridge the Divide

Courtney Plotts, Ph.D.

COPYRIGHT 2020

Author	Courtney Suzanne Plotts, Ph.D.
Publisher	DBC Publishing Sandston, VA
ISBN	978-1948149174
Cover Art	2020© DBC Publishing / Courtney Suzanne Plotts, Ph.D.

Author: You may contact the author with questions, comments, or continuing research inquiries at courtneyplottsphd@gmail.com

Table of Contents

Table of Figures 4

Forward 5

Dedication 6

Chapter 1 – Exploring the Canyon: What We Do in Online
Spaces 7

Chapter 2 – Cultural Canyon Geography of Online Spaces
.... 17

Chapter 3 – Building a Bridge Across the Canyon 31

Chapter 4 – LatinX Learning Preferences Insight in the
Canyon 41

Chapter 5 – Building Bridges Across the Canyon 47

Chapter 6 – The Canyon and Framework(s) Connecting 61

Chapter 7 - Conclusion 77

Index 81

References 85

About the Author 93

About The Book 94

Table of Figures

Figure 1 - Big Vision Questions For The Cultural Canyon of LatinX Students 13

Figure 2 - Community of Inquiry Image: Terry Anderson/Marguerite Koole, 2013© 18

Figure 3 - Online Model For Community Engagement and Student Success of LatinX Students In Online Spaces Plotts, 2018© 20

Figure 4 - Faculty Teaching Standards for Online Spaces: LatinX Students 32

Figure 5 - Teaching and Learning With Cultural Learning Lens 44

Figure 6 - Current Model of Online Learning for LatinX Students 62

Figure 7 - Successful Outcomes for LatinX Students with Contextual and Collaborative Learning............................ 62

Figure 8 - Culturally Responsive Educator View 64

Forward

You are teaching in higher education. You were thrust into teaching online. The barriers were substantial for you and your students … from the technology, planning, and connecting with students … to the fatigue of being in online meetings.

Sadly, we changed or lost connections with our students and our faculty. The circumstances also forced us to look at specific aspects of online teaching to develop our skills more effectively in online spaces.

The year 2020 helped us realize that online spaces were more important than originally thought. Culturally competent teaching is just as important in online settings as it is in face-to-face settings.

Genuine student connections and culturally responsive teaching in online spaces require intentionality and a prevention mindset. This book provides practical insight and evidence-based, skill-building for online spaces – specifically for the culture of LatinX students. The purpose of this book is to help instructors apply culturally-responsive teaching in online spaces for LatinX students.

Dedication

This book is dedicated to the pursuit of justice, listening, learning, equality and understanding in higher education. To the people, families, to the friends, and communities of Latino/a, LatinX, Hispanic and Indigenous people. To the undocumented who live in fear while obtaining education globally online.

To the LatinX community and LatinX leaders doing amazing work:

- Nohemy Ornelas, VP of Academic Affairs
- Yvonne Teniente-Cuello, Dean, Student Services and Her Team
- Héctor Álvarez, Faculty and Counselor
- Melissa L. Salazar, Ph.D., Escala Education
- Liddy Wartwig, An amazing Brazilian wife, mom, and friend.
- Margarita Olvera, Hardee County Schools, Secretary to the director of ESE services a role model and unsung hero for LatinX students in rural America.
- Natalie Cardona, The best example of social justice warrior. Thank you for all you do!

and

- Flower Darby, who understood and saw the value and importance of my vision for this work

Chapter 1

Exploring The Canyon:
What We Do In Online Spaces

The word 'canyon' comes from the Spanish word cañon, which means a tube or pipe. A 'cultural canyon' is a measurable disconnect in the perception pipeline between the ethnic culture of a student group and the learning culture of an institution. Cultural canyons occur when a host culture (higher education) differs significantly from the student culture. In this case – the LatinX culture. Like physical canyons, cultural canyons are built through the process of erosion. Attributes of an academic online culture erode aspects of motivation, well-being, belongingness, and self-identity among LatinX students.

Communication, caring, and connection flow through cultural canyons. If we try to communicate with a group of people standing on the other side of a canyon, specific outcomes are expected:

1. Bad reception. The line of communication is not clear.
2. Echo. The same information is repeating with no end in sight. Yet, the echo does not change the

meaning of the words spoken or the behavior of people on the other side of the canyon.

3. Wind. Fast wind through a canyon can be deafening.
4. Silence. Because the canyon divide is too wide for you to hear the sound.

This analogy highlights experiences that LatinX students have in online spaces. A cultural canyon is contributing to LatinX students' challenges in online spaces.

How well does your institution communicate across the canyon to LatinX students? Most institutions respond by saying, "We do a good job of working with LatinX students." However, those colleges do not have the data to prove this case in online spaces. Higher-education institutions put forth their best effort in practices that work against desired outcomes for improving communications with LatinX students.

One assumption found in higher education culture is LatinX culture is a consideration added to the teaching and learning *process*, rather than a *foundation* of learning. After all of the individualist, task-oriented, transactional, and learning task boxes are checked for the online space, consideration for LatinX culture is *sometimes* considered and applied as an after-thought in the teaching and learning process.

This system can keep us from understanding:

- The important role LatinX culture plays in the learning process in online spaces.
- The true size of the divide between the online and LatinX culture.
- The strong contribution of cultural competency training programs and what they contribute to LatinX student experiences in online spaces.
- How LatinX students navigate online spaces and the instructor's implementation for course design.

Why is this important for higher education?

"Researchers have emphasized the need for educational reform to support the academic reality of Latino students in the United States" (Maldonado-Torres, 2014, p.14).

Exploring what we are doing and why it is not working is critical to improving academic success of LatinX students in online spaces. Higher-education institutions announce their work towards continuous improvements for LatinX programming. Oftentimes, in the online space, improvements are not included in these continuous efforts. These institutions describe their process to steps similar to what is listed below:

1. Identify observable increases in LatinX students.
2. Implement cultural programming on residential campuses through student services.
3. Take last year's diversity plan and update it for larger academic discrepancies.

4. Submit the plan for state, local, and/or federal funding.
5. Hope that the academic progress changes.
6. Next year, repeat steps 1-5 again.

Faculty members and administrators in higher education fail to see the 'big picture' of why LatinX students are unsuccessful in online spaces. In this book, the author builds a framework for the importance of LatinX culture in the learning experiences of those LatinX students, as well as formulas that contribute to the best teaching and learning practices for LatinX students, in online spaces. After reading this book, faculty (professors, trainers, and instructors) should be able to build a bridge across the cultural canyon of online learning. More specifically, this book will:

• Introduce the role of LatinX culture, its relationship to learning psychology, and the framework of its importance for online settings.
• Support faculty development and understanding of successful learning experiences for LatinX students (rather than an afterthought of their teaching process).
• Present a model of best practices for faculty teaching LatinX students in online spaces.
• Provide a practical framework for faculty to think about, develop, and apply to their online course through the lens of cultural and academic success.

- Present culturally-responsive teaching methods targeted towards the LatinX student success in online spaces.

The following concepts work together as the foundations of the bridges to be built across cultural canyons. Understanding the framework for online teaching and learning of LatinX students is dependent on a basic understanding of the following terms:

Cultural Lens - The Cultural Lens Approach (CLA) applies a cultural framework to psychological and learning experiences (Hardin et al., 2014). Cultural context alters the application of psychological theory (Hardin et al., 2014; Triandis, 1994; 1996). Behaviors, experiences, and cognitions are viewed through the appropriate lens of ethnic culture when CLA is applied by researchers (Hardin et al., 2014). CLA includes two assumptions: 1) culture-specific knowledge is required to expand any existing psychological theory because each individual experiences the world with a cultural framework, therefore 2) allowing for the universal applications of psychological theory when applied to human behavior and the mental process (Hardin et al., 2014).

Psychological Experiences "involve the aspect of intellect and consciousness experienced as combinations of thought, perception, memory, emotion, personal will, and imagination, including all unconscious cognitive processes. The term can refer, by implication, to a thought process. Psychological experiences are framed by ethnic culture (Mental Experience, 2019, para 1.).

Social Experiences are determined to be the result of cognitive and practical activities of the individual, manifested in the synthesis of knowledge about the social reality, experiences of performing the methods of activity, and experiences of emotional relationships (Safronova, 2014). Social experiences are influenced by culture.

Learning Experiences "refers to any interaction, course, program, or other experience in which learning takes place, whether in traditional academic settings (schools, classrooms) or nontraditional settings (outside-of-school locations, outdoor environments), or whether it includes traditional educational interactions (students learning from teachers and professors) or nontraditional interactions (students learning through games and interactive software applications)" (Anonymous, 2019, para.3). Learning experiences are influenced by culture.

Figure 1 - Big Vision Questions For The Cultural Canyon of LatinX Students

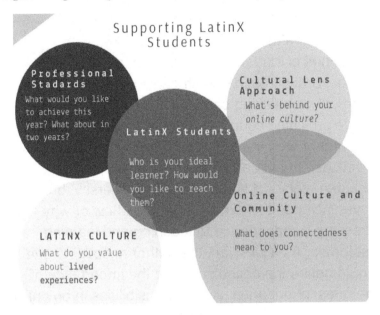

Psychological, social, and educational experiences occur within online-learning environments. The factors that drive LatinX students to successful learning experiences are rooted in cultural norms and psychological, social, and educational constructs associated with LatinX culture.

Faculty want to improve online experiences for LatinX students. To assist instructors, this book explores the psychological and social factors through a cultural lens. LatinX students' academic successes are heavily reliant on LatinX cultures' influence on the psychological and social perceptions in online spaces.

How did this work come about?

The author has always been fascinated by culture. For almost 12 years, she worked with thousands of students in online spaces. Most were first-generation LatinX or African-American students in an online teaching capacity or in a clinical virtual space providing counseling or clinical assessment. The author was given guidelines for best-teaching practices, and in each incidence, the guidelines included a blanket statement about diversity, but never included the extra-steps of the how or why – or stressing its importance to teaching and learning outcomes. As a clinician, the author noticed no one would define the online space or the importance of the rules, boundaries, and responsibilities in an online space for clinical practitioners. When the author was the Program Director at Esperanza College in Philadelphia, she noticed the LatinX culture was front and center in the face-to-face environment, but there was significant resistance to online learning for both faculty and students.

As the National Chair for the Council For At-Risk Student Education and Professional Standards, the author's work involved consulting on projects that focused on first-generation, college students and their academic success. The projects were initially devoid of cultural consideration. This work with student success led to an ongoing focus to assist faculty by providing a framework for success across ethnic cultures.

The author wanted a methodology that was academically sound for faculty that would also support thriving learning communities for students. A big piece of this work included the important aspects of academic and ethnic culture. The framework describes how we use the aspects of humanness in online spaces and the role that culture plays in that experience. This book builds within each chapter to provide a robust understanding of LatinX culture and its role in online spaces.

The Structure of This Book

Chapter 2 looks at two theoretical foundations of academic success of LatinX in online spaces: The Community of Inquiry Theory and the Cultural Lens Approach.

Chapter 3 presents a set of professional standards for faculty which outlines the important aspects of online learning significantly influenced by ethnic culture; in this case, LatinX culture.

Chapter 4 explores the experiences of LatinX learners in online spaces. The chapter illustrates the barriers and boundaries that online learning culture presents for LatinX students, as well as LatinX student learning preferences.

Chapter 5 provides pre-planning discussion questions to be used for self-discussion and discovery or with peers and teaching colleagues.

Chapter 6 looks at pulling all of the aspects together to provide rigorous, robust, and culturally responsive academic experiences for LatinX students in online spaces.

Chapter 7 concludes with brief, take-away points.

Chapter 2

Cultural Canyon Geography and Online Spaces

Historically, researchers applied the Cultural Lens Approach (CLA) to academic learning and testing (Triandis, 1994), cognition and behavior (Schutt, Allen, & Laumakis, 2009), group dynamics (Paletz, Miron-Spektor, & Lin, 2014), cross-cultural psychology (Hardin et al., 2014), and personality (Laher, 2013). Additionally, researchers investigated the validity of academic-assessment items developed for standardized testing using CLA (Triandis, 1996). Researchers wanted to determine the level of test-item equivalence among different cultural groups. The interpretation of written communication was found to be unique among specific ethnic groups (Triandis, 1996).

The Community of Inquiry Theory (Garrison, Archer, & Anderson, 2000). This theory is the most widely used theory in online learning. The Community Inquiry Theory (CIT) is made up of three separate constructs: cognitive presence, teaching presence, and social presence. Cognitive presence is how actively engaged both learners and faculty are in online spaces with one another. Teaching presence is how available the teacher is and how masterful they are at delivering content in online space.

Figure 2 - Community of Inquiry Image: Terry Anderson/Marguerite Koole, 2013©

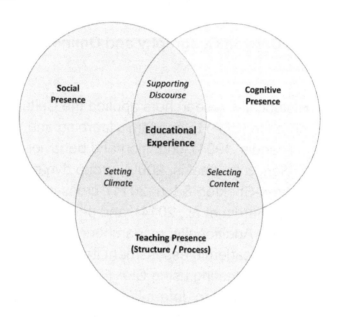

Social presence is a psychological attribute of how people connect in online spaces. The current literature suggests that instructors create social presence through specific behaviors associated with communication. Immediacy, interactivity, and authenticity are cited as conduits of building a social presence. Social presence has been associated with positive psychological outcomes for marginalized students. It increases a sense of belonging and decreases the sense of isolation.

Academic literature discusses the psychological importance of social presence for online students. Psychological facets include perceptions of a sense of community, sense of belongingness, sense of well-being, and connectedness. Yet, the individualistic culture of online learning does not align with the psychological attributes when viewed through a cultural/ethnic lens.

Although researchers highlight these aspects as being important to the online-learning process, these attributes are developed, perceived, and maintained differently among ethnic groups through cultural norms and values. The perception of social presence is also heavily influenced by culture, cultural norms, and values often associated with individual cultural and ethnic groups.

Building and maintaining a social presence for LatinX students requires the use of the Cultural Lens Approach. Faculty need to apply the CLA with intentionality, investment, and understanding. LatinX students attending higher education institutions in the United States benefit from the intentional and mindful application of the CLA in online-space (virtual) teaching practices. This is because LatinX students filter their individual perceptions of online (learning) experiences through a cultural lens.

Figure 3 - Online Model For Community Engagement and Student Success of LatinX Students In Online Spaces Plotts, 2018©

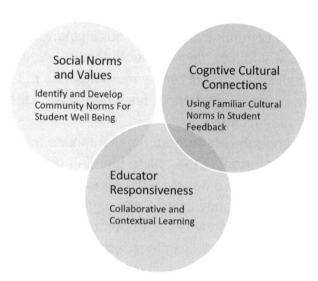

Online-learning experiences include social experiences, learning experiences, and cognitive experiences. These experiences occur through a cultural lens. For faculty, the cultural lens may include differences between the face-to-face campus environment versus the online (virtual) campus. For students and the faculty, it could seem to be the same, but it may also include differences associated specifically with ethnic culture. Because ethnic culture(s) influences psychological outcomes associated with academic success, teaching online – using CLA – is critical to the LatinX students' success.

Applying CLA to understanding best-teaching practices and student experiences increase positive outcomes for LatinX students. The following list of research conclusions demonstrates the important relationship between the LatinX student culture and implementing a CLA approach in online (education) spaces:

- Contextual learning is a type of social learning that uses the environment to assist in obtaining information associated with cultural norms (Migliorini, Rania, & Cardinali, 2015).
- Collaborative learning supports the academic achievement of LatinX students (Maldonado-Torres, 2014).
- LatinX students benefit from collaborative learning experiences (Maldonado-Torres, 2014).
- LatinX students use collaborative experiences to support language and culture development and group norms (Hachey, Wladis, & Conway, 2014).
- Researchers found ethnic and cultural consideration increased course attendance and individuals' participation (Booker, Merriweather, & Campbell-Whatley, 2015).
- LatinX students use contextual learning to position themselves within a social group (Sirin, Ryce, Gupta, & Rogers- Sirin, 2013).
- Online-learning experiences including e-portfolios, online mentorships, and highly-trained faculty who specialize in e-learning and ethnicities, resulting in positive outcomes for LatinX online learners (McNair, Finley, Duhig, McCambley, Brown, Santiago, & Gonzalez, 2014).

- Multiculturalism is a positive feature of online-learning experiences (Dzumbinski, 2014).

Responding to the contextual learning preferences of LatinX students requires culturally-responsive teaching practices. Culturally responsive teaching is important for a variety of reasons. First, online culture differs from face-to-face campus culture. Students need time to adjust to that cultural difference.

Second, the psychological attributes associated with successful outcomes of LatinX students in online spaces are dependent on culturally-specific cues in the online learning environment. When such cues are not perceivable, LatinX students struggle to connect and thrive in online spaces.

Third, the lack of consideration for LatinX culture in the online-learning space can increase psychological and social barriers to successful academic outcomes. The consideration of culture in online spaces is arguably more important than in face-to-face spaces. Online environments are often void of psychological and social cues associated with successful outcomes for LatinX students. This void includes the inability to view the body language, facial expressions, reactions, and/or hear voice inflections of educators and peers.

Online learning has its own culture. Online-learning culture is comprised of three parts: online-learning culture (individualistic), residential and campus culture (academic), and ethnic culture (norms and values) of the individuals within the online space. The online-learning culture has attributes associated with online learning, which include individualism, self-motivation, and self-efficiency. The residential campus culture is often individualistic. It includes campus and course policies and procedures, student services, and academic advising – often presented as something sought by individuals. Each of these cultural dynamics contributes to the experiences of LatinX students in online spaces.

The following lists of academic research point out conclusions that demonstrate the influence of culture on the psychological and social aspects of online learning:

Online Learning and Community Psychology

- A sense of community refers to the perception of belongingness and mutual commitment of individuals in a collective unity (McMillan & Chavis, 1986).
- Social justice is "fair and equitable resources, opportunities, and obligations within a community" (Dalton, Ellis, and Wanderman, 2001, p.16).
- Citizen/learner participation refers to the peaceful, respectful, collaborative process of community members to have meaningful involvement within the community (Prilletensky, 1999).
- The boundaries of a community and the sense of commonality include psychological, social, and cultural considerations from all members within a

diverse learning community (Van de Vijver et al., 2015).

- Including consideration for ethnic perspectives on social presence contributes to the increase of communal perceptions and behaviors (Soper & Ukot, 2016).

Online Learning and Social Psychology

- Group development is essential for collaborative and contextual learning experiences (Borokhovski, Bernard, Tamim, Schmid, & Sokolovskaya, 2016).
- Online instructors construct and manage online group development for students (Brame & Beil, 2015).
- Cross-cultural psychologists suggested that a sense of community did not occur through one standard of expectations or framework, but rather through the ethnic perspectives of its members (Van de Vijver et al., 2015).
- The definition of respect, and how respect is perceived and is reciprocated, differs among various ethnic groups (National Institute of Health, 2016).
- The online learning environment is associated with (its own) cultural attributes and expectations (Gaytan, 2013).
- A barrier to online acculturation is writing proficiency (Luyt, 2013). Online-learning experiences include a culture that places significant value on one's literacy levels and

writing ability (Luyt, 2013). This includes proper syntax, grammar, and sentence structure (Luyt, 2013). LatinX students often struggle with proficiency in both literacy and written language (Johnson-Ahorlu & Cuellar-Mejia, 2014).

- Acculturation in online learning spaces is significantly more difficult because online learning and socialization requires high levels of literacy and writing proficiency to be successful (Luyt, 2013).

Online Learning and Mental Health

- Prior experiences with isolation diminish LatinX learners' ability to experience academic acculturation positively, thus decreasing the satisfaction of socialization and social support (Ashlong & Commander, 2015) in online-learning environments.
- LatinX participants were more likely to have suicidal ideations after experiencing acculturative stress by way of perceived or actual discrimination (Lawton & Gerdes, 2014).
- LatinX students struggle with periods of depression, PTSD, and anxiety while in a post-secondary learning environment (Stebleton, Soria, & Huesman, 2013).
- According to Posselt & Lipson (2016), anxiety and depression increased for marginalized populations

when perceived stereotypes about class and ethnicity were present.

- "In some cases, LatinX may cope with mental-health issues by seeking advice from friends, family members, or spiritual advisers and may not seek help from mental health professionals. In other cases, there is a lack of understanding and knowledge regarding mental health, which increases the stigma associated with mental illness" (Anonymous, 2020, p.3).
- Some LatinX students will select marginalization as a method of coping with acculturative stress because of past experiences with stereotyping or racism within the host culture (Castillo, Navarro, Walker, Schwartz, Zamboanga, Whitbourne, Weisskirch, Kim, Park, Vazsonyi, & Caraway, 2015).
- Acculturation and acculturative stress contribute to depression differently for male and female LatinX college students (Castillo et al., 2015).

Current Best Practices Excluding Cultural Consideration

- Video conference experiences of some ethnic minority students resulted in frequent miscommunication and negative student experiences associated with isolation and exclusion (Snowball, 2014).

- Threaded discussion boards led to feelings of isolation for ... LatinX learners (Luyt, 2013).
- A team's ability to build unity among team members is dependent on collaboration and its value among each group member's ethnic or cultural group (Zhao, Sullivan, & Mellenius, 2014).

Cultural Psychology and Online Learning

- LatinX students experience violations of their cultural norms and values when attending higher education institutions (Ojeda, Castillo, Meza, R., & Piña-Watson, 2014).
- LatinX students perceive racism and macro-aggression in online settings more frequently than in face-to-face settings (Barraclough, & McMahon, 2013).
- Online environments are full of cultural canyons due to unknown applications of unintentional micro-aggressions by instructors ... supported through individualistic online culture (Luyt, 2013).
- LatinX student experiences include cultural conflict with online culture, limited pathways to build a sense of community, and racial bias from educational leadership (Ojeda et al., 2014).

Cultural Lens Approach: Values For Online Spaces

- One's value of diversity is dependent on a variety of factors associated with cultural competency (Booker et al., 2015).
- Faculty should develop socio-emotional and culturally relevant interpersonal communication in the learning environment (Campbell, 2014).
- Intentionality is a critical piece for planning, building, and maintaining connectedness in online spaces (Soper & Ukot, 2016).
- CLA is considered a behavioral motivating tool for student's academic success.
- Face-to-face communication provides supplemental information that supports emotional and contextual learning and understanding, often not available in online environments (Lundberg & Sheridan, 2015).
- Successful online collaboration is … associated with one's perception of ethnic self-identity (Altugan, 2015).
- Dzumbinski (2014) posited cultural competency did not occur automatically, but only occurred if an intentional effort was made by faculty and their administration.

LatinX perceptions of psychological and social exchanges in online spaces are tied to a cultural lens. The aforementioned points of interest highlight the reasons why faculty should want to consider adding a CLA to their teaching practice. LatinX culture is a conduit for socialization, belongingness, emotional support, and positive, academic outcomes. The exclusion of LatinX CLA in instructional design and teaching practice creates significant barriers to healthy social, psychological and academic outcomes in online spaces of students identifying with the LatinX culture.

Chapter 3

Building A Bridge Across the Canyon

Faculty members aware of cultural canyons may want to create a 'connectedness' across the canyon. The task may seem overwhelming, but it doesn't have to be. Faculty thrive when clarity and clear directions are provided. Altering or improvement of teaching practices requires a professional mindset. Standards help faculty members increase student learning across the board. An important question for faculty to ask themselves is:

What professional standards have I been following when working with LatinX students in online spaces?

Professional standards are important because they promote and guide educational practice for faculty teaching practices. For faculty teaching online for the first time, standards provide a pathway to exploring and applying best practices and effective teaching strategies for specific student populations. The Council For At-Risk Student Education and Professional Standards (2017) developed faculty

teaching standards for faculty teaching at Hispanic
Serving Institutions.

Figure 4 - Faculty Teaching Standards for Online Spaces: LatinX Students

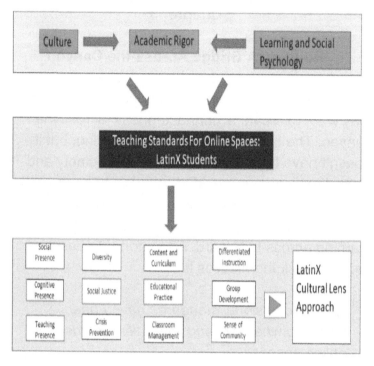

These standards are developed within a
Cultural Lens Approach (CLA) (Hardin, et al., 2014)
and the Community of Inquiry Theory (Garrison et al.,
2000). These professional standards identify 13 areas
of teaching standards for LatinX students in online
spaces. The following outline of the noted standards
will assist in creating a framework for the skills faculty
can develop through this book and application of
these techniques.

The following professional teaching standards and aligned with the academic success of LatinX students in online spaces:

Educational Professional Practice - A qualified educator skilled in CLA and cultural competency will utilize appropriate skills to build and maintain academic, social, and psychological well-being, while delivering educational content in an online space to the same quality or greater than in face-to-face environments. Educators are expected to follow the same ethical scope of educational practice in online spaces, as in face-to-face educational practice. Faculty members will complete a CASEPS Certification Training Program for the focused population, LatinX.

Curriculum and Content - Faculty will furnish the appropriate content and assessment materials in online spaces with equitable access for students. This may include, but is not limited to, virtual assessments, handouts, synchronous / asynchronous academic support, curriculum guidance, and educational interventions. For LatinX students, faculty will use content and assessment methods that align with the best practices of contextual and collaborative-learning experiences.

Classroom Management - Faculty will facilitate and manage acceptable academic and social behavior in online spaces with a global consideration for academic and LatinX cultural norms.

Differentiated Instruction - Faculty will be skilled in providing different CLA (LatinX) methodology for explaining content within the online space. This may include, but is not limited to, lectures, small group, one-on-one instruction, visual, audio, or other methods of learning.

Online Climate - Faculty are responsible for the creation and maintenance of the student experience in a virtual platform (video conferencing software, e.g., Google Hangouts, Zoom, WebEx, Dox.net) for discussion forums, announcements, and asynchronous video sessions, with the understanding of how LatinX student culture may influence these experiences.

Sense of Community - When working in online classes, the faculty will foster, develop, and maintain a sense of community within the online space with LatinX cultural considerations. Traditionally, the term 'sense of community' refers to the level to which an individual perceives interaction between one's self and other community members in an online setting. In an online environment, a sense of community is often built through the frequency of interaction, immediacy of interaction, and consistency of interaction with students (Borup, West, & Thomas, 2015). Faculty members will add best practices associated with LatinX cultural-community norms and values when creating a sense of community in an online space.

Group Development - Developed by Tuckman and Jensen (1977), group development is a theoretical model that fosters collaboration and meaningful outcomes among group members (Raes, Kyndt, Decuyper, Van den Bossche, & Dochy, 2015). This model of group development is frequently used to explain and explore small group dynamics in online learning and social exchanges (Kumar, Deshmukh, & Adhish, 2014). The development and maintenance of online groups fosters interpersonal skills and social welfare among group members. Group development is essential for social learning in online spaces through collaborative experiences of group members (Borokhovski, Bernard, Tamim, Schmid, & Sokolovskaya, 2016). When working with online groups, faculty will support group development in the online space using a CLA lens and make intentional consideration for LatinX-cultural norms and values when creating team groups, assignments, and expectations.

Teaching Presence - Teaching presence consists of three components: design, facilitation of discourse, and direct instruction to occur through a cultural lens" (Beck, 2015, para. 3). Faculty working with LatinX students will use LatinX cultural norms as a conduit for presenting novel ideas and new conceptual knowledge in the online space. The faculty member will develop and maintain teaching presence with intentionality for ethnicity and equity of access to curriculum and instructor interpersonal communication.

Social Presence - Social presence refers to the psychological experience and attributes of online environments (Garrison et al., 2010; Plante & Asselin, 2014; Short & Christie, 1976). Social presence is also the psychological attribute of authenticity, genuineness, and transparency. Social presence refers to the psychological experience and attributes of online environments (Garrison, Archer & Anderson, 2010; Plante & Asselin, 2014; Short & Christie, 1976). Social presence is the essence of care and connectedness in online spaces (Plante & Asselin, 2014).

The faculty member will develop and maintain a social presence with all appropriate aspects of cultural considerations. This will occur through the under-standing of caring as perceived through a specific LatinX ethnic group. In other words, a faculty member is doing their best to convey their genuineness through the ethnic lens of the student in addition to their own understanding and norms of caring behaviors.

Cognitive Presence - The faculty member will generate and actively facilitate cognitive presence through the CLA. Faculty members will use LatinX culture to build meaning for concepts through the lens of LatinX culture. Cognitive presence is the extent to which the participants within an online space are able to construct meaning through sustained communication (Garrison et al., 2000). In other words, the faculty will be fully emotionally and cognitively present within the session and limiting any activities that can distract or take away from the facilitation of education, unless extreme measures are warranted (e.g., clinical emergencies that require student-service interventions or calls to 911).

Diversity - Faculty members will demonstrate a respect for diversity and multiculturalism in online spaces. Building social presence varies among different ethnic groups (Aronson & Laughter, 2015; Soper & Ukot, 2016). Including consideration for ethnic perspectives contributes to building or increasing communal perceptions and behaviors (Soper & Ukot, 2016). Diversity considerations support the socialization process in online spaces (Dzumbinski, 2014). Consideration of diversity supports the acculturation process of moving students from face-to-face to online-learning environments and minimizes marginalizing experiences for students transitioning to online environments from site-based schools (Campbell, 2015; Carter, 2015; Heightener & Jennings, 2016; Lawton & Gerdes, 2014).

Crisis Intervention - Faculty members will be able to apply crisis prevention and intervention skills in online spaces. "Crisis intervention involves three components: 1) the crisis, the perception of an unmanageable situation; 2) the individual or group in crisis; and 3) the faculty member, the helper, or mental health worker who provides aid. Crisis intervention requires the person experiencing crisis receive timely and skillful support to help cope with his/her situation before future physical or emotional deterioration occurs" (Stevens & Ellerbrock, 1995, P.1). LatinX students experience higher levels of isolation and depression in online spaces than their counterparts. Crisis prevention and intervention is critical to the safety and well-being of LatinX students in online spaces.

Social Justice - Online faculty members will seek out and develop fair and equitable practices within the online space. Faculty will possess an understanding that social justice is also applicable to personal relationships (Dalton et al., 2002) and demonstrate an awareness for social justice issues that are important to student well-being and sense of community.

Multiculturalism is a positive feature of online-learning experiences (Dzumbinski, 2014). Understanding the important standards associated with successful outcomes for LatinX students helps faculty understand the boundaries and parameters of what is expected in online spaces. Faculty members may feel overwhelmed at the thought of meeting the educational preferences of various ethnic groups. The feeling contributes to negative mental-health outcomes for both faculty and students.

Providing faculty with an outline of what is expected for meeting the needs of LatinX students in online spaces creates a pathway for faculty to develop their teaching skill sets including cultural responsiveness. To place a greater value on cultural competency and its role in online spaces, the aforementioned standards are outlined to support faculty in thinking about how and where they would like to focus their culturally responsive teaching and learning practices in their online course space. Standards provide guidelines as well as a foundation for building culturally-responsive teaching and learning experiences with LatinX students.

Chapter 4

LatinX Learning Preferences:
Insight in the Canyon

LatinX cultures are collectivist in its nature. A collectivist culture is one that focuses on a 'sense of connectedness' rather than an individual within the group. LatinX student learning experiences differ from their European-American counterparts (Maldonado-Torres, 2014). Unlike their European-American counterparts, who prefer individualistic learning experiences (Freeman & Huang, 2015; 2014), collaborative and contextual learning experiences are preferred by LatinX learners (Maldonado-Torres, 2014).

Collaborative learning is a type of social learning that engages students with their peers (Higher Education Report, 2014). Contextual learning is a type of social learning that uses the environment to assist in obtaining information associated with cultural norms (Migliorini, Rania, & Cardinali, 2015). Collaborative learning supports academic achievement of LatinX students (Maldonado-Torres, 2014). LatinX students use collaborative experiences to support language and culture development and group norms (Hachey et al., 2014). Collaborative experiences for LatinX students, which includes both native Spanish speakers and native English speakers, resulted in positive academic and social outcomes for LatinX students (Hachey et al., 2014). Collaborative experiences provide an opportunity for LatinX students to experiment with different learning styles (Fogg, Carlson-Sabelli, Carlson, & Giddens, 2013).

Contextual learning is also a preference of LatinX students (Maldonado-Torres, 2014). Contextual learning includes reflective observation and concrete learning experiences associated with higher levels of LatinX student satisfaction (Maldonado-Torres, 2013). The LatinX community encompasses significant cultural differences among ethnic nationalities.

Maldonado-Torres (2013) explored the relationship between specific cultures and learning preferences and found significant differences between students of Dominican ethnicity and students of Puerto Rican ethnicity regarding preferences of concrete learning (e.g., including real world applications). Concrete learning was preferred more by Puerto Rican students than by Dominican students (Maldonado-Torres, 2014). Such results suggested that ethnicity and national culture contributed to the selection of psycho-educational approaches to learning among LatinX students.

LatinX students use contextual learning to position themselves within social groups (Sirin et al., 2013). LatinX students select unique learning preferences – and learning preferences are influenced by ethnicity (Maldonado-Torres, 2014). Both contextual and collaborative learning are preferences for LatinX students (Maldonado-Torres, 2014).

Online-learning experiences including e-portfolios, online mentorships, and faculty that were highly trained and specialized in e-learning and ethnicity, which resulted in positive outcomes for LatinX online learners (McNair, Finley, Duhig, McCambley, Brown, Santiago, & Gonzalez, 2014). More specifically, within the context of both collaborative and contextual learning, LatinX students reported positive outcomes associated with technology when it assisted them with language barriers in online classes (Johnson-Ahorlu & Cuellar-Mejia, 2014).

Although both collaborative and contextual learning opportunities provide psychological and social support in the learning environment (Migliorini et al., 2015). LatinX students experience negative outcomes associated with online-learning experiences (Johnson & Cuellar-Mejia, 2014). These researchers noted the achievement gap between both LatinX students and their European-American peers widened in online-learning environments by almost half. The researchers posited this was due to limited access to technology associated with online learning including internet service, computers, and technology skills (Johnson & Cuellar-Mejia, 2014). However, Thompson et al. (2013), found that pathways to

building teacher-student relationships were
significantly lower in the online environment and
directly contributed to the academic disparities
between LatinX students and their European-
American counterparts. Such experiences influence
the psychological, academic, and social factors
associated with successful outcomes of LatinX
students (Zvolensky, Jardin, Garey, Zuzuky, & Sharp,
2016).

Figure 5 - Teaching and Learning With Cultural Learning Lens

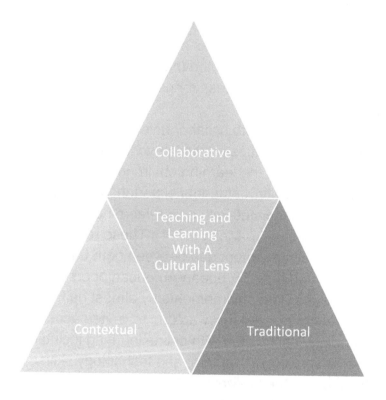

Additionally, most online instructors' ethnic culture aligns with the online learning culture. Online instructors need high levels of cultural responsiveness (Soper & Ukot, 2014) when working with LatinX students in an online space. European-American assumptions and stereotypes of other ethnic groups influence content and delivery (Grant & Lee, 2014) is associated with the community of inquiry theory (Garrison et al., 2000). Barriers to building relationships are influenced by human perception and ethnocentricity (Booker et al., 2015). Ethnocentricity is a set of beliefs one uses regarding his or her own race and culture to justify its significance over another group (Hammerich, 2014). This definition implies an intentional act. That implication is a powerful one and one that may prevent European-American faculty from fully embracing culturally-responsive teaching practices. It may be the academic culture, not their own ethnic culture, is a factor that contributes to the disconnection between LatinX students and the online space. Or ... perhaps it is the individualistic nature of the academic and online culture that the faculty member has adopted.

Researchers have linked ethnocentricity with educational experiences of LatinX students (Hammerich, 2014). Researchers suggest, when LatinX faculty were available to teach the course (Hachey et al., 2013), academic outcomes improved compared to their European-American counterparts due to cultural awareness and responsiveness. Learning experiences for LatinX students are may be limited in or devoid of LatinX faculty because faculty are often reflective of European-American student groups (Madyun Williams, McGee, & Milner IV, 2013). This is not to suggest that only LatinX faculty should be teaching LatinX students, but to highlight the importance of LatinX culture in the teaching and learning process.

LatinX students' culture supports specific preferences for learning styles. These learning styles need to be considered when instructional planning occurs. The culturally responsive educator will use the information in this chapter to add cultural depth to their lesson planning. Contextual and collaborative learning build specific and culturally-relevant pathways for LatinX students to access and understand content knowledge.

Chapter 5

Building Bridges Across the Canyon

Planning is a critical part of successful learning outcomes for students in online spaces. Reflection is an important part of the planning process when attempting to build a bridge of culturally responsive teaching for LatinX students. The following section of this book uses the professional standards outlined in Chapter 3 to provide context for discussion questions. These questions can be used as a personal reflection or with peers in a professional learning or community setting.

Educational Professional Practice

Foundation Principle: Culturally responsive teaching includes intercultural exchanges occurring within the collaborative experiences (Dzubinski, 2014). Cultural exchange requires a recognition of the host culture (higher education) of the cultural norms and expectations of the non-host culture (LatinX culture) to be successful (Demes & Geereat, 2014). Questions to ask when teaching LatinX students online:

1. What set of professional standards have I been following when educating LatinX students?
2. Where do I want to start? How can I apply the standards in Chapter 3 to my online class?
3. When planning and designing a course, how often do I consider ethnic culture as a factor in my planning, course development, and content development process?
4. How might the standards provided in Chapter 3 help me develop and implement my teaching practices?

Curriculum and Content

Foundation Principle: Perceptions of irrelevant curriculum content decreases one's ability to sense social presence (Cunningham, 2015). Culture plays a significant role in one's ability to perceive social presence and academic outcomes in online spaces (Carter, 2015; Cunningham, 2015; Dzumbinski, 2014; Soper & Ukot, 2016). Online course development and online teaching requires appropriate emphasis on culturally sensitive curriculum and teaching and learning practices (Aronson & Laughter, 2015). Questions to ask when teaching LatinX students online:

1. How might my curriculum development be enhanced by adding LatinX CLA?

2. When developing curriculum, how often is cross-cultural curriculum explored within the content area, e.g., curriculum from another HSI or culture?

3. Review a part of a curriculum you developed in the past. Does it include contextual and collaborative learning goals, exercises, assignments or outcomes?

Classroom Management

Foundation Principle: "The most significant value shared across LatinX culture is the importance given to family unity, welfare, and honor. There is a deep sense of family commitment, obligation and responsibility. A stable expectation of LatinX culture is ... when a person is having problems, others will help, especially those in stable positions" (McGoldrick, Giordano, Garcia-Pretro, 2005, p.162). Eliciting, listing, and validating stories about how their (LatinX students') lives are affected in the online environment help individuals' problem-solve complex individual or family issues (McGoldrick et. al., 162). Questions to ask when teaching LatinX students online:

1. Revisit your classroom policy. Does this policy highlight the important cultural aspects that may conflict with online or academic culture?

2. Does your classroom policy note the importance of family obligation?

3. When you review excused and unexcused assignments, does it align with the cultural norms of LatinX culture?

Differentiated Instruction

Foundation Principle: Contextual learning was also associated with cross-cultural experiences that build self-esteem among LatinX students. Contextual learning provides opportunities for LatinX students to apply their personal values and meanings to social exchanges (McGoldrick et al., 2005). A strong self-identity within a cultural context is critical to successful online-learning experiences (Altugan, 2015). Questions to ask when teaching LatinX students online:

1. List all of the various ways you introduce material in the online space. Which of these align with contextual or collaborative learning practices?
2. How might you present or introduce material in a storytelling or narrative method?
3. How do you differentiate your instruction in the online space?
4. What skills would you like to develop to enhance your instruction within your online course?

Online Climate

Foundation Principle: Researchers suggest that acculturation (Booker et al., 2015; White & Ali-Khan, 2013) and marginalization, (Eckland, 2013; Ojeda et al., 2014; Oberts, 2015) contribute to feelings of isolation (Eckland, 2013; White & Ali-Khan, 2013) among LatinX students in online spaces. Questions to ask when teaching LatinX students online:

1. If you were invited to a colleague's home for a dinner party, how would you want to feel when you entered their space?
2. Is that the same feeling you are attempting to create for your LatinX in the online space? What might you need to add to your online course to help increase the feeling of belonging for LatinX students?
3. What information could you send to your students prior to the start of the course that would help them understand the tone of your classroom climate?
4. How are you making sure students are comfortable enough in the boundaries of the online community?

Diversity

Foundation Principle: Ethnic identity and cultural norms significantly contribute to a student's ability to be successful in online environments (Bryant & Bates, 2015; Campbell, 2015; Carter, 2015; Grant & Lee, 2014; Snowball, 2014). Acculturative stress is defined as "the abrupt or enforced entry into a different and unknown cultural environment" (Brailas, Koskinas, Dafermos, & Alexias, 2015, p. 62), thus creating a psychological struggle to find social and personal balance within a novel group culture. LatinX students struggle to adapt to European-American cultural norms associated with academic culture. This is because the practices of European-American culture do not psychologically align with some of the values and norms of the LatinX culture (Johnson & Galy, 2014). Questions to ask when teaching LatinX students online:

1. How might acculturative stress be impacting your LatinX students prior to entering an online space?
2. What are your perceptions of how well LatinX students are adjusting to the online environment?
3. What assumptions, if any, might you have made in the past about how your students are assimilating into the online space?
4. How might those assumptions be misaligned with what you have learned so far about LatinX students in online spaces?

Sense of Community

Foundation Principle: Cultural inclusivity creates a sense of community and belongingness among different ethnic groups (Hoshiar, Dunlap, Li, & Friedel, 2014), while cultural exclusivity leads to feelings of isolation and depression (Stebleton et al., 2014). Cultural belongingness is associated with academic achievement of LatinX students (Jury, Smedding, Court, & Darnon, 2014). Questions to ask when teaching LatinX students online:

1. What are the values and norms you want to emphasize in your online learning community? How are your students made aware of those values and norms? How are you sharing those values with students?
2. How might those values align or conflict with LatinX cultural norms?
3. On a scale of 1 to 10 (10 being very important), how much do you value a sense of community in your personal and professional life?
4. If you asked your students to grade the sense of community in the online space, would it reflect that same score? Why or why not?

Teaching Presence

Foundation Principle: Effective online instructors provide models of appropriate content and syntax as a way to increase the quality of social presence in online environments (Mykota, 2015). Instructor and peer modeling provide guidelines for student participation (Bryant & Bates, 2015; Dzumbinski, 2014). Instructor modeling increased the likelihood of student online participation and interaction with student peers and the instructor (Mbati and Minnaar, 2015). Questions to ask when teaching LatinX students online:

1. Name three areas in your online course where you model expectations and outcomes.
2. How can you increase your modeling of academic behaviors for LatinX students in online spaces?
3. How might you want to improve how you are selecting curriculum, applying teaching methodology, and/or focusing discussions in your online class?

Social Presence

Foundation Principle: Online instructors are responsible for constructing 70% or more of the social presence in the online space (Mbati & Minnaar, 2015; Plante & Asselin, 2014). Cultural competency training is critical for successful online teaching and learning experiences. Dzumbinski (2014) explored the role of culture in online environments and found online teaching of ethnic minority groups requires alternative strategies for building multicultural social contexts. Questions to ask when teaching LatinX students online:

1. When building connections with your students, what role does your culture play in that process? What role does LatinX culture play in the process?
2. How do students know you care? Is your 'caring behavior' interpreted through your cultural lens or the lens of LatinX students?
3. How have you demonstrated caring in the past? Now that you know about cultural differences in the expression of caring, what might you change about your communication with your LatinX students?
4. What attributes of caring do you want to ensure are conveyed in your online space?
5. How might you use spoken narratives to increase student content knowledge?
6. How can you use storytelling in your online course, to help people understand the content you are teaching?
7. Where can you add narrative teaching and learning experiences?

Cognitive Presence

Foundation Principle: "Cognitive presence is central to successful student learning. The quality of cognitive presence reflects the quality and quantity of critical thinking, collaborative problem-solving, and construction of meaning occurring in student-to-student and student-to-faculty interactions. You can model and support cognitive presence in your interactions with students in discussions, assignment feedback, and other communications" (Types of Presence: Cognitive and Social, n. d.). Questions to ask when teaching LatinX students online:

1. How might you use LatinX cultural norms and values to foster inquiry, exchange information, and connect ideas?
2. How are you expressing value and norms you have created or are present with in the online course as it relates to teaching and learning?

Group Development

Foundation Principle: LatinX students use contextual learning to position themselves within a social group (Sirin, et al., 2013). Group development is essential for collaborative and contextual learning experiences to occur (Borokhovski, Bernard, Tamim, Schmid, & Sokolovskaya, 2016). Online instructors construct and manage online group development for students (Brame & Beil, 2015). Online facilitators often construct groups alphabetically, randomly, or a mixed group of high performing and low performing students (Brame & Beil, 2015). Once teams are assigned or formed, the process of group development begins (Cheng, Nolan, & Mcaulay, 2013). Online group development occurs without consideration for cultural norms of each member (Chin, 2013). Questions to ask when teaching LatinX students online:

1. What grouping strategies do you use in your online courses when creating teams? How might LatinX cultural norms influence those practices?
2. When building content for team assignments, are the team expectations individualist or collective?
3. How might current conflict resolution policy violate cultural norms of LatinX student understanding group/team assignments?
4. Apply CLA to that policy. How has that policy changed?

Social Justice

Foundational Principle: Social Justice: "The tradition of liberation psychology in Latin America represents one example of the psychological pursuit of social justice ... this includes enabling individuals to use their 'voice' to articulate their own experiences. The social justice movement is also associated with individual empowerment" (Dalton et al., 2002, p.17). Questions to ask when teaching LatinX students online:

1. Historically, has social justice been part of your community values in your online space? If so, how did you demonstrate or convey that within the course?
2. What might you want to add to your community policy to support social justice causes or the general importance of social justice issues?
3. Is social justice something you are willing to add to your community values in the online space? Why or why not?

Crisis Prevention

Foundation Principle: "Common mental health disorders among LatinX are generalized anxiety disorder, major depression, post-traumatic stress disorder (PTSD) and alcoholism. While LatinX communities display a similar susceptibility to mental illness as that of the general population, they experience health disparities that affect the way they receive mental health care, such as the access and quality of treatment. Only 20% of Latinos who experience symptoms of a psychological disorder talk to a doctor about their symptoms, and only 10% contact a mental health professional" (Anonymous 2020, para. 3).

A large barrier to treatment is that in the Hispanic community, as with other ethnic minority groups, talking about emotions is not a common part of the culture, so treatments such as cognitive behavioral therapy alone are not effective. There is a lack of understanding and knowledge regarding mental health, which increases the stigma associated with mental illness. Language is also a barrier as many medical professionals do not speak Spanish, and those that do speak the language may not understand the cultural issues that Latinos face.

Other barriers include lack of health insurance, legal status, and misdiagnosis" (Anxiety and Depression Association of America, 2020, para.3). Questions to ask when teaching LatinX students online:

1. What is the campus plan for online crisis prevention?
2. Do you know how to implement that policy in an online space for a LatinX student that may have a language barrier?
3. What questions might you ask your administrator regarding crisis prevention, policy, and procedure before you teach your next course?
4. What document can you ready for students that may contain but is not limited to resources that address:

   a. Domestic Violence
   b. Alcoholism
   c. Mental Health

    d.   Housing Assistance

    e.   Self-Harm

Organized and meaningful reflection is critical to improving instructional outcomes. Thinking about how one plans and prepares the online space is directly associated with how well our LatinX students connect to that space. Intentionality preparing online learning spaces is critical for the academic success of LatinX students in online spaces.

The purpose of this chapter was to help faculty members working with LatinX students reflect on the practices they have been applying in online spaces and how those practices may or may not be as meaningful for LatinX students in online spaces.

Chapter 6

Using Framework(s) To Cross The Canyon

Using the foundation of the learning and social psychology research, and combining it with the Cultural Lens Approach (CLA), the following framework was developed to support successful learning experiences for LatinX students in online spaces. The current best practices associated with online learning include psychological, social, and behavioral attributes not filtered through the cultural lens of LatinX students. Faculty who improve their culturally responsive teaching practice contribute to successful outcomes for LatinX students in online spaces.

Figure 6 - Current Model of Online Learning for LatinX Students

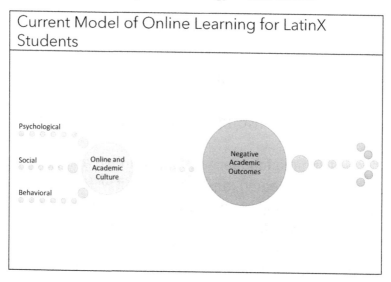

*Figure 7 - Successful Outcomes for LatinX Students with Contextual and
Collaborative Learning*

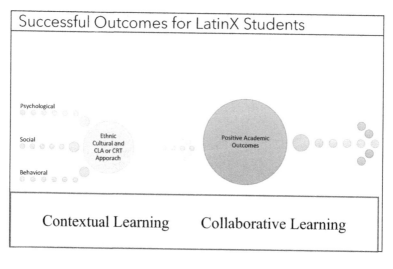

Assumptions associated with the success of this model.

- Faculty are willing to explore and adapt their teaching practices.
- Faculty understand the importance of the standards presented in this book.
- Faculty have completed culturally responsive CASEPS Teaching Practices Certification for LatinX students 2016[©].
- Faculty understand some of the obvious as well as nuanced differences between LatinX ethnic groups.

Ignoring the important role of ethnic culture in the learning process leads to Eurocentric values that translate to oppressive perspectives and experiences for Non-European-American students (Booker et al., 2015). Campbell (2015) suggested that non-implementation of culturally-responsive teaching increases the potential for discrimination and acculturative stress in learning experiences. Culturally-responsive teaching addresses specific ethnic and cultural aspects of online-learning experiences (Heightner & Jennings, 2016). The absence of cultural competency limits learning experiences of ethnic-minority groups in online learning (Campbell, 2015). Culturally responsive teachers directly contribute to the well-being of minority populations in online spaces. See figure 8.

Figure 8 - Culturally Responsive Educator View

Culturally Responsive Educator View: The Relationship Between Learning Experiences and Student Success
✓ Culturally Responsive Teaching (CRT) is a prevention measure for academic failure associated with acculturative stress. ✓ CRT requires intentionality on the part of the instructor. ✓ CRT does not equate to a decrease in academic rigor. ✓ CRT is a required and perfected skill of a master educator. ✓ CRT helps students develop a sense of community in an online space and behaviors associated with academic success. ✓ CRT helps students develop a stronger sense of self-identity in an online space.

Online-faculty members are the facilitators, builders, maintainers, and sustainers of relationships among members of the learning community within the framework of culturally responsive teaching methodology (Soper & Ukot, 2016). Building a culturally-inclusive atmosphere requires an understanding of community members and their ethnic and cultural norms (Dzubinski, 2014). Online-learning environments are limited on ethnic and cultural cues (Brailis et al., 2016). Carter (2015) found individuals could identify ethnicity in virtual spaces because ethnic exchanges are associated with specific levels of 'intensity.' This allows people to ethnically identify one another and relate to one another, while also creating a strong self-identity within online spaces (Prause & Mujtaba, 2015). A culturally responsive classroom facilitator is able to recognize these attributes to build and sustain healthy collaborative and social experiences in a learning environment (Heightner & Jennings, 2016).

General Understanding of LatinX Culture

Over the years, the researcher has provided a variety of professional developments that focus on the skill-building of online faculty for first-generation, college-student populations. The writer has highlighted best practices associated with LatinX students.

In general, the LatinX culture is mostly communal and family-centered. LatinX students place significant value on immediate and extended family - including godparents. Children are also valued in the LatinX culture. Geopolitical trauma often shapes the experience of LatinX students. Those experiences and cultural norms and values have shaped the preferences for learning novel concepts (McGoldrick et al., 2005).

The following outline of cultural and ethnic norms will help faculty sharpen their cultural lens for LatinX students in online spaces. This is not an exhaustive list; however, it is a list to assist faculty in connecting with their LatinX students online and various aspects of interpersonal communication. The list is adapted from McGoldrick et al., (2005) for interpersonal communication and dynamics of LatinX's cultures.

This framework assists in bridging the cultural canyon that exists between LatinX students and their academic experiences in online spaces. Conceptualize the differences in culture and how it may be impacting your communication, sense of community, and connectedness with your LatinX students in online spaces.

Best Practice #1: Develop and plan courses with LatinX culture in mind.

Online Cultural Lens For Course Design: Best Practices For Course Design (CourseArk, 2020, para. 3.)

- Include features in the course that assesses students' learning at every stage.
- Use multiple-choice quizzes instead of essay assessments, which are very hard to evaluate in an asynchronous learning environment.
- Add assessments, following short segments of learning material, rather than just at the end of the course.

- Provide immediate feedback on assessments, rather than several weeks later or only at the end of the course.
- Refrain from just offering Pass/Fail or Correct/Incorrect types of feedback. Your corrective feedback should include details of why the answer was correct or incorrect, with optional additional content / resources the learner can access.

LatinX Group Cultural Lens Best Practices For Course Design

Contextual Learning

- *Brazilian* Cultural Lens: Storytelling, Social Games, Problem Solving
- *Central American* Cultural Lens: Cause and Effect Learning, Before and After Scenarios with exploration of its importance and reflection.
- *Columbian* Cultural Lens: Skill Building and Application
- *Cuban* Cultural Lens: Problem Solving Activities
- *Dominican* Cultural Lens: General Concept Linkage Instead of Specifics
- *Mexican* Cultural Lens: Mapping, Classification, and Content Relationships
- *Puerto Rican* Cultural Lens: Allusion, Proverbs, and Parables

Best Practice #2: Culture Equals Caring.

Online Cultural Lens For Caring Behaviors:
"Faculty messages that are respectful, positive, encouraging, timely, and frequent will foster social presence and caring behaviors, while also allowing for caring interactions, mutual respect, and finding meaning in relationships." (Plant and Asselin, 2014, p.4).

Online LatinX Cultural Lens For The Expression Of Care In Online Spaces:

- *Brazilian* Cultural Lens: Validation of the culture is critical to demonstrate caring.
- *Central American* Cultural Lens: Extending and receiving forgiveness is central to perceptions of caring behaviors.
- *Columbian* Cultural Lens: Students perceive investment in personal skill building as a caring act.
- *Cuban* Cultural Lens: Demonstrate care by showing the importance to the process of problem-solving skills.
- *Dominican* Cultural Lens: Praise of physical attributes of things like jewelry, clothing, etc.
- *Mexican* Cultural Lens: Instructor intentionality of stability and consistency – within the online space – demonstrates care.

- *Puerto Rican* Cultural Lens: Demonstrate concern and understanding for feelings of disrespect when presented by students.

Best Practice #3: Apply Cultural Mindfulness Before Communicating Course Policy.

- *Brazilian* Cultural Lens: Genuineness flows through the construct of concern for family.
- *Central American* Cultural Lens: Expect delays at times in response due to immigration status concerns.
- *Columbian* Cultural Lens: Family loyalty is paramount.
- *Cuban* Cultural Lens: Self-problem-solving is most likely.
- *Dominican* Cultural Lens: Social empathy is required for behavioral change associated with assignment submission.
- *Mexican* Cultural Lens: Course absences occurs most frequently when instructor does not respect the role of family values and its values.
- *Puerto Rican* Cultural Lens: Least likely LatinX group to ask for help from peers or outsiders.

Best Practice #4: Build policy that includes culturally relevant access to healthcare.

Online Cultural Lens: If a student suffers from a critical situation and/or medical or family emergencies, the student can file a class absence notification request with the Student Emergency Services in the Office of the Dean of Students. After this, the student's professors will be notified of the student's condition. This does not apply to non-emergencies, according to the Dean of Students, which includes illnesses such as cold, flu, staph infection, and mononucleosis. Students with these issues must contact the professors directly"
(Liu & Bolf, 2018, para. 1).

Online LatinX cultural lens for online absence (medical issues) documentation policy

- *Brazilian* Cultural Lens: Students do not like being dependent on resources or people for help. Fear of being a burden and not self-dependent. May not seek medical or psychological treatment as other LatinX groups.
- *Central American* Cultural Lens: Face significant barriers to accessing medical care.
- *Columbian* Cultural Lens: Significant access to medical care and extended resources when compared to their counterparts.

- *Cuban* Cultural Lens: Significant access to medical care and extended resources.
- *Dominican* Cultural Lens: Face significant barriers to accessing medical care. May reference *curanderismo* (folk healer)
- *Mexican* Cultural Lens: Intentionality of stability and consistency within the online space. May reference *curanderos* (folk healer)
- *Puerto Rican* Cultural Lens: Least likely to seek outside medical treatment.

Best Practice #5: Provide feedback that is academically and culturally relevant.

Online Cultural Lens For Providing Feedback

"Many students have mentioned to us that online courses can be intimidating because of the isolated nature that often comes with online classes. Recently, students in our online courses completed reflections concerning learning in an online environment. A common theme within the reflections was the feeling of being *connected to a community because they had the comradery of their peers combined with the support of their instructor.* They specifically attributed this feeling to the meaningful feedback provided throughout the course" (Rottman & Rabidoux, 2017, para. 8).

Online LatinX Cultural Lens For Providing Student Feedback

- *Brazilian* Cultural Lens: The feedback should reflect the cultural value of self-reliance.
- *Central American* Cultural Lens: The feedback should reflect the cultural value of a sense of mastery.
- *Columbian* Cultural Lens: The feedback should reflect the cultural value of education and resourcefulness.
- *Cuban* Cultural Lens: The feedback should reflect the cultural value of individual problem-solving skills.
- *Dominican* Cultural Lens: The feedback should reflect the cultural value of the physical presentation of the assignment.
- *Mexican* Cultural Lens: The feedback should reflect the cultural value of the cohesion and harmony presented within the context of the assignment.
- *Puerto Rican* Cultural Lens: Provide feedback in the context of respect for the course or material provided.

Best Practice #6: Build culturally responsive policy for team assignments.

Online Learning Cultural Lens: "In most instances, group work in online courses is cooperative at best.

Small group exchanges within online courses were examined and discussed in the paper, 'How much *group* is there in online group work,' where students interactions were categorized as: 1) parallel, 2) associative, and 3) cooperative interactions (Lowes, 2000, p. 4). Only one group of the five examined approached the higher level of cooperation" (Morrison, 2014, para. 1).

Online LatinX Cultural Lens Team Development

- *Brazilian* Cultural Lens: Understanding and validation is critical to preventing and reducing conflict in team spaces.
- *Central American* Cultural Lens: May disregard team assignments all together, due to the lack of trust fostered among team members.
- *Columbian* Cultural Lens: Strong and consistent negotiation skills are a tool used to navigate collaborative experiences.
- *Cuban* Cultural Lens: Least likely to report team issues. Individualistic problem-solving more likely.
- *Dominican* Cultural Lens: May not participate in live video sessions due to the value of appearance and the timing of the team collaboration. Personal approach is a deeply importance cultural value.
- *Mexican* Cultural: Indirect, implicit, and cover communication is focused on getting along and group harmony.

- *Puerto Rican* Cultural Lens: Open differences of opinion and demands for clarification are seen as rude and insensitive.

What Next?

With the best intentions, faculty contributions in online spaces get lost in the cultural canyons. We discuss the need to personalize aspects of online teaching such as academic feedback, yet we omit one of the most personal aspects of people; cultural identity. The best practices and considerations presented in this chapter contribute to diminishing the wind, echo, and silence in the cultural canyons of online spaces for LatinX students and their educators.

Applying culturally responsive teaching practices in all teaching and instructional spaces within a teaching practice can feel like an overwhelming. For faculty members feeling overwhelmed by the prospect of culturally responsive teaching practices – select one area of focus, i.e. feedback, sense of community, and/or discussion – and build from there.

The examples presented in this chapter will help teachers bridge the cultural canyon between LatinX students and connections in online spaces. Faculty course preparation usually includes the creation of assignments, the development of courses, and writing of syllabi. Prior to academic planning, faculty should outline their strategy for creating connectedness in online spaces. Strategic planning for genuine student and instructor connection adds a meaningful dimension to online spaces. Take the time to reflect on how you, as a teacher, are connecting with your students and their needs. Our faculty voices will travel across the canyon if we are intentional about the communication and connecting with students in online spaces.

It should be noted that student's personality, previous educational experiences, and environmental circumstances may influence cultural norms and their uses. This chapter presents small examples and considerations to be added to what instructors are already doing to enhance student engagement. For full understanding and application of these practices, faculty and instructors may want to attend the associated training and professional development opportunities suggested in this book.

A note about Salvadorian culture and other ethnic groups within Latin culture: At the time of this book, there was not enough research to include Salvadorans, as well as any other ethnic group that is not listed. As soon as that information is available it will be added to the second edition of this book.

Chapter 7

Conclusion

The lack of cultural understanding about LatinX students significantly impacts psychological attributes associated with successful online learning experiences. In Chapter 1, the author identified the meaning of cultural canyons. In Chapter 2, the author explored online learning theory and the influence of culture on those theoretical frameworks. In chapter 3, the author explored the professional standards aligned with online teaching for LatinX students. In chapter 4, the author explored the LatinX experience in online spaces. In chapter 5, the author discussed the importance of planning. In chapter 6, the author reviewed the overall picture of the importance of LatinX consideration in online culture. In chapter 7, current best practices were provided and a cultural lens was applied to those practices for various LatinX groups.

This book has outlined the importance of LatinX culture and its influence on the online teaching and learning process. Should you want a quick list of take-aways that you can share with your administration, co-workers, or your students see points below.

- Do not underestimate the power of LatinX culture in the learning process.
- Successful learning is grounded in understanding academic and ethnic culture.
- Take time to participate in your class as a student, not just as a teacher.
- Define what community means to you and how you can express that in your student's online learning space.
- Explore the role of an online diversity officers and their role in online courses.
- Increase cultural competency training focusing on online spaces.
- It is the intentional things that make the biggest difference.

The author is dedicated to improving online academic spaces for all students. This is a small contribution to the teaching and learning practices associate with the academic successes and appropriate support for LatinX students in online spaces.

INDEX

academic acculturation ... 25

academic assessment 17

academic learning 17

acculturative stress .. 25, 26, 52, 63

Alcoholism 59

anxiety 25, 58

Assumptions 63

Bad reception 7

barriers5, 15, 22, 29, 43, 59, 70, 71

behavior 8, 11, 17, 33

belongingness 7, 19, 23, 29, 53

Best Practice 66, 68, 69, 70, 71, 72

Brazilian . 67, 68, 69, 70, 72, 73

campus plan 59

cañon

  canyon 7

Cause Related Marketing

  CRM 2

*Central American*67, 68, 69, 70, 72, 73

citizen/learner participation 23

Classroom Management 33, 49

clinical assessment 14

cognition 17

cognitive presence... 17, 36, 56

Cognitive Presence... 36, 56

collaboration . 27, 28, 35, 73

Collaborative learning 21, 41

collectivist 41

Columbian.... 67, 68, 69, 70, 72, 73

communal behaviors 24

communal perceptions... 24, 37

community members 23, 34, 64

Community of Inquiry

  Theory 15, 17, 32

computers 43

Concrete learning 42

content development 48

contextual learning... 21, 22, 24, 28, 41, 42, 43, 56

Contextual learning.. 21, 41, 42, 50

Contextual Learning........ 67

Council For At Risk Student Education and Professional Standards 14

course development 48

Crisis Intervention 37

crisis prevention 37, 59

cross-cultural psychology 17

*Cuban*67, 68, 69, 71, 72, 73

cultural awareness.......... 45

cultural canyon.. 7, 8, 10, 66

Cultural canyons 7

cultural competency ... 9, 28, 33, 39, 63, 78

cultural context 50

cultural lens.. 13, 19, 20, 29, 55, 61, 65, 77

Cultural Lens 11, 15, 17, 19, 28, 32, 61, 67, 68, 69, 70, 71, 72, 73, 74

Cultural Lens Approach CLA 11, 15, 17, 19, 28, 32, 61

Cultural Mindfulness Before Communicating Course Policy 69

cultural norms 13, 19, 21, 27, 34, 35, 41, 47, 50, 52, 53, 57, 64

cultural programming 9

cultural responsiveness .. 39

cultural understanding..... 77

culturally responsive teaching ... 22, 39, 45, 47, 61, 63, 64

culture 2, 5, 7, 8, 11, 12, 14, 15, 17, 19, 20, 21, 22, 23, 24, 26, 29, 36, 41, 42, 45, 46, 47, 48, 49, 52, 55, 59, 65, 66, 68, 75, 78

Culture Equals Caring..... 68

curriculum 36, 48, 49

Curriculum and Content. 33, 48

depression ... 25, 26, 38, 53, 58

Differentiated Instruction 34, 50

discrimination 25, 63

diversity ... 10, 14, 28, 37, 78

Diversity 37, 52

diversity plan 10

Domestic Violence 59

Dominican.... 42, 67, 68, 69, 71, 72, 73

Echo................................ 8

educational interactions .. 12

Educational Professional Practice 33, 47

educational reform 9

Ethnocentricity 45

Eurocentric values 63

Expression Of Care In Online Spaces 68

face-to-face settings. 5

faculty 5, 10, 11, 14, 15, 17, 20, 21, 28, 29, 31, 32, 33, 34, 35, 36, 38, 39, 43, 45, 56, 60, 64, 65

Foundation Principle 47, 48, 49, 50, 51, 52, 53, 54, 56, 58

Garrison, Archer, & Anderson

Garrison, Archer, & Anderson............. 17

Geopolitical trauma......... 65

group development.. 24, 35, 56

Group Development.. 35, 56

group dynamics 17, 35

health disparities............. 58

higher education culture ... 8

higher education institutions 19, 27

Housing Assistance 60

human perception........... 45

instructional design 29

internet service 43

interpersonal communication 28, 36, 66

isolation.. 18, 25, 26, 27, 38, 51, 53

language 21, 22, 25, 41, 43, 59

LatinX culture 7, 8, 9, 10, 13, 14, 15, 21, 29, 36, 47, 49, 52, 55, 65, 66, 77, 78

LatinX students 5, 7, 8, 9, 10, 11, 13, 15, 16, 19, 21, 22, 25, 26, 27, 31, 32, 33, 35, 38, 39, 41, 42, 43, 45, 46, 47, 48, 49, 50, 51, 52, 53, 54, 55, 56, 58, 59, 60, 61, 63, 65, 77, 78

learning community .. 24, 53, 64

learning environment 22, 24, 25, 28, 43, 65, 66

Learning Experiences 12, 64

learning preferences 15, 22, 42, 43

learning styles 42, 46

literacy 24, 25

macro-aggression 27

Mental Health 25, 59

mental health care 58

mental health issues 26

mental health professional 58

mental health professionals 26

mental illness 26, 58, 59

Mexican .. 67, 68, 69, 71, 72, 73

miscommunication 26

model 10, 35, 54, 56, 63

models 54

motivation 7

Multiculturalism 22, 38

Online Absence / Documentation Policy . 70

online acculturation 24

Online Climate 34, 51

Online Cultural Lens For Course Design 66

online culture .. 7, 16, 22, 27, 45, 77

online environments. 28, 36, 37, 52, 54, 55

online settings 5, 10, 27

online spaces 5, 8, 9, 10, 11, 13, 14, 15, 16, 17, 18, 22, 28, 29, 31, 32, 33, 35, 37, 38, 39, 47, 48, 51, 52, 54, 60, 61, 65, 77, 78

online teaching 5, 11, 14, 48, 54, 77

personality 17

planning ... 5, 16, 28, 46, 47, 48, 77

posttraumatic stress disorder

PTSD 58

professional developments 65

Providing Feedback 71

Providing Student Feedback 72

psychological cues 22

psychological exchanges 29

Psychological Experiences 11

psychological theory 11

PTSD 25

posttraumatic stress disorder 58

Puerto Rican 42, 67, 69, 71, 72, 74

racism 26, 27

Salvadorian 75

self-identity 7, 28, 50, 64, 65

sense of community. 19, 23, 24, 27, 34, 53, 64, 66

Sense of Community 34, 53

Silence 8

social cues 22

social exchanges 29, 35, 50

social experiences 20, 65

Social Experiences 12

social groups 42

social justice.. 23, 38, 57, 58
Social Justice 38, 57
social media 2
social presence .. 17, 18, 19,
   24, 36, 37, 48, 54, 68
Social Presence 36, 54
social support 25, 43
socialization 25, 29, 37
stereotypes 26, 45
stigma 26, 59
successful learning
   outcomes 47
suicidal ideations 25
synthesis of knowledge ... 12

teacher-instructor
   relationships 44
teaching practices.... 14, 19,
   20, 22, 31, 45, 48, 63
teaching presence 17, 35
Teaching Presence... 35, 54
teaching training 61
Team Development 73
teams 57
technology 5, 43
technology skills............. 43
virtual space................... 14
virtual spaces................. 65
well-being........ 7, 19, 33, 38
Wind................................. 8

References

Altugan, A. S. (2015). The effect of cultural identity on learning. *Social and Behavioral Sciences, 190,* 455-458. doi:10.1016/j.sbspro.2015.05.025

Aronson, B., & Laughter, J. (2015). The theory and practice of culturally relevant education: A synthesis of research across content areas. *Review of Educational Research, 86,* 163-206. doi.org/10.3102/0034654315582066

Anonymous (2020, March 22). LatinX. Anxiety and Depression Association of America. https://adaa.org/hispanic-latinos

Anonymous (2017, April 26). Learning experience. https://www.edglossary.org/learning-experience/#:~:text=Learning%20experience%20refers%20to%20any,whether%20it%20includes%20traditional%20educational

Aronson, B., & Laughter, J. (2015). The theory and practice of culturally relevant education: A synthesis of research across content areas. Review of Educational Research, 86 (1), 163-206. doi.org/10.3102/00346543155582066

Barraclough, L., & McMahon, M. (2013). U.S. Mexico student's online collaboration. Transformative learning across power and privilege. Equity and Excellence in Education. 46(2) 236-251.

Booker, K. C., Merriweather, L., & Campbell-Whatley, G. (2016). The effects of diversity training on faculty and students' classroom experiences. *International Journal for the Scholarship of Teaching and Learning, 10,* 1-7. doi:10.20429/ijsotl.2016.100103

Borokhovski, E. Bernard, R. M., Tamim, Schmid, R. F. & Sokolovskaya, R. M. (2015). Technology supported student interaction in post-secondary education. A meta-analysis of designed versus contextual treatment. *Computers and Education, 96* DOI: 10.1016/j.compedu.2015.11.004

Borup, J., West, R. E., & Thomas, R. (2015). The impact of text versus video communication on instructor feedback in blended courses. Educational Technology Research and Development, 63, 161–184. doi.org/10.1007/s11423-015-9367-8

Brailas, A., Koskinas, K., Dafermos, M., & Alexias, G. (2015). Wikipedia in education: Acculturation and learning in virtual communities. *Learning, Culture and Social Interaction, 7,* 59-70. doi.org/10.1007/s11423-015-9367-8

Brame, C. J., & Biel, R. (2015). Setting up and facilitating group work: Using cooperative learning groups effectively. Retrieved from http://cft.vanderbilt.edu/guides-sub-pages/setting-up-and-facilitating-group-work-using-cooperative-learning-groups- effectively/.

Bryant, J., & Bates, A. J. (2015). Creating a constructivist online instructional environment. *TechTrends, 59,* 17-22. doi.org/10.1007/s11528-015-0834-1

Campbell, E. (2015). Transitioning from a model of cultural competency toward an inclusive pedagogy of "racial competency" Using critical race theory.

Journal of Social Welfare and Human Rights, 3, 9-27.
doi.org/10.15640/10.15640/jswhr.v3n1a2

Carter, E. V. (2015). Delivering "virtual ethnicity" Drama: A pedagogical design
for bridging digital and diversity barriers. *American Journal of Business
Education, 8,* 327-348. doi.org/10.19030/ajbe.v8i4.9425

Castillo, L. G., Navarro, R. L., Walker, J. E. O. Y., Schwartz, S. J., Zamboanga,
B. L., Whitbourne, S. K., Weisskirch, R. S., Kim, S. Y., Park, I. J. K.,
Vazsonyi, A. T., & Caraway, S. J. (2015). Gender matters: The influence of
acculturation and acculturative stress on Latino college student depressive
symptomatology. *Journal of Latina/o Psychology, 3*(1), 40–55.
https://doi.org/10.1037/lat0000030

Cheng, X., Nolan, T., & Macaulay, L. (2013). Don't give up the community: a
viewpoint of trust development in online collaboration. *Information
Technology & People, 26,* 298–318. doi.org/10.1108/ITP-10-2012-0116

CourseArk, (2020, February 23). Best practice for online course design.
https://www.coursearc.com/best-practices-for-online-course-
design/Cunningham, J. M., (2015). Mechanizing people and pedagogy:
Establishing social presence in the online classroom. *2015, 19*(3), 1-14.
Retrieved from http://olj.onlinelearningconsortium.org

Dalton, J. H., Ellas, M. J., & Wandersman, A. (2005). *Community psychology.
Linking individuals and communities.*

Demes, K. A., & Geeraert, N. (2013). Measures matter: Scales for adaptation,
cultural distance, and acculturation orientation revisited. *Journal of Cross-
Cultural Psychology, 45,* 91- 109. doi.org/10.1177/0022022113487590

Dzubinski, L. M. (2014). Teaching presence: Co-creating a multi-national online
learning community in an asynchronous classroom. *Journal of
Asynchronous Learning Network, 18*(2),97-113. Retrieved from
http://sloanconsortium.org/publications/olj_main

Ecklund, K. (2013). First-generation social and ethnic minority students in
Christian universities: Student recommendations for successful support of
diverse students. *Christian Higher Education, 12,* 159-180.
doi.org/10.1080/15363759.2011.598377

Experience, Mental (2020, January 13). In Wikipedia. Retrieved from
https://en.wikipedia.org/wiki/Experience#cite_note-4

Freeman, R., & Huang, W. (2014) Collaboration: Strength in diversity.
International Journal of Science, 515, 305. doi.org/ doi:10.1038/513305a

Freeman, R. B. & Huang, W. (2015) Collaborating with people like me: Ethnic co-
authorship within the US. Journal of Labor and Economics, 33, 289-318.
doi:10.1038/513305a

Fogg, L., Carlson-Sabelli, L., Carlson, K., & Giddens, J. (2013). The perceived
benefits of a virtual community: Effects of learning style, race, ethnicity, and
frequency of use on nursing students. *Nursing Education Perspectives, 34,*
390-394. doi.org/10.5480/11-526.1

Garrison, D. R., Anderson, T., & Archer, W. (2000). Critical inquiry in a text-
based environment: Computer conferencing in higher education model. *The
Internet and Higher Education, 2*(2-3), 87-105. Retrieved from
https://www.journals.elsevier.com/the-internetand-higher-education/

Garrison, D. R., Anderson, T., & Archer, W. (2000). Critical inquiry in a text-
based environment: Computer conferencing in higher education model. The
Internet and Higher Education, 2(2-3), 87-105. Retrieved from
https://www.journals.elsevier.com/the-internetand-higher-education/

Hammerick, K. (2014). Commentary on framework for multicultural education.
Journal of *Canadian Chiropractic Association.* 58(3) 280-285.

Hardin, E. E., Robitschek, C., Flores, L. Y., Navarro, R. L., & Ashton, M. W.

(2014). The cultural lens approach to evaluating cultural validity of
psychological theory. *American Psychologist, 69*, 656-668.
doi:10.1037/a0036532

Hachey, A. C., Wladis, C., & Conway, K. M. (2014). The representation of
minority, female, and non-traditional STEM majors in the online environment
at community colleges: A nationally representative study. *Community
College Review, 43*, 89-114. doi:10.117/0091552114555904

Heightner, K. L., & Jennings, M. (2016) Culturally responsive teaching knowledge
and practices of online faculty. *Online Learning, 20*(4) 54-78. Retrieved from
https://olj.onlinelearningconsortium.org/index.php/olj/article/view/1043

Hoshiar, M, Dunlap, J., Li, J., Friedel, J. N. (2014). Examining the effectiveness
of student authentication and authenticity in online learning at community
colleges. *Community College Journal of Research and Practice, 38*, 337-
345. doi:10.1080/10668926.2012.755649

Johnson-Ahorlu, R. N. & Cuellar, M. (2016). Examining the complexity of the
campus racial climate at a Hispanic serving community college. *Community
College Review, 44*, 135- 152. doi.org/10.1177/0091552116632584

Johnson, J., & Galy, E. (2013). The use of e-learning tools for improving Hispanic
students' academic performance, Journal of Online Teaching and Learning,
9(3), 328-341.Retrieved from http://jolt.merlot.org

Jury, M., Smeding, A., Court, M., & Darnon, C. (2015). When first-generation
students succeed at university: On the link between social class, academic
performance, and performance- avoidance goals. *Contemporary
Educational Psychology, 41*, 25-36. doi:10.1016/j.cedpsych.2014.11.001

Kumar, S., Deshmukh, V., & Adhish, V. S. (2014). Building and leading teams.
Indian Journal of Community Medicine, 39, 208-213. doi:10.4103/0970-
0218.143020

Laher, S. (2013). Understanding the five-factor model and five factor theory
through a South African Cultural Lens. *South African Journal of Psychology,
44*, 208-221. doi:10.1177/0081246313483522

Lawton, K., & Gerdes, A., (2014). Acculturation and Latino adolescent mental
health. Integration of individual, environment, and family influences. *Clinical
Child and Family Psychology Review, 17*, 385-398. doi.org/10.1007/s10567-
014-0168-0

Lundberg, C. A. & Sheridan, D., (2015). Benefits of engagement with peers,
faculty, and diversity for online learners. College Teaching 63(1) 8-15.

Lui, J. & Bolf, M. (2018). Sick? Your syllabus doesn't care. Retrieved from
https://thedailytexan.com/2018/10/14/sick-your-syllabus-doesnt-care

Luyt, I. (2013). Bridging spaces: Cross-cultural perspectives on promoting
positive online learning experiences. *Journal of Educational Technology
Systems, 42*, 3-20. doi:10.2190/ET.42.1.b

Maldonado-Torres, S. E. (2014). The relationship between Latino students'
learning styles and their academic performance. *Community College
Journal of Research and Practice, 38*, 357-369.
doi.org/10.1080/10668926.2012.761072

Maldonado-Torres, S. E. (2013). Differences in learning styles of Dominican and
Puerto Rican students. We are Latinos from the Caribbean; Our first
language is Spanish; Our learning Preferences are different. *Journal of
Hispanic Higher Education.* 10(3) 226-236.

Madyun, N., Williams, S.M., McGee, E.O. & Milner IV, H. R., (2013). On the
importance of African American Faculty in Higher Education. Educational
Foundations Summer Ed.

Mbati, L., & Minnaar, A. (2015). Guidelines towards the facilitation of interactive
online learning programmes in higher education. *International Review of*

Research in Open and Distance Learning, 16, 272-287.
doi.org/10.19173/irrodl.v16i2.2019

McGoldrick, M., Giordanio, J., & Garcia-Preto, N., (2005). Ethnic and family
therapy. Guilford Press. McMillan, D.W. & Chavis, D. M. (1986). Sense of
community: Definition and theory. Journal of Community Psychology, 14, 6-
23.

McNair, T. B. Finley, A. Duhig, C., McCambley, H. Brown, S. Santiago, D. &
Gonzalez, A. (2014). Finding what works for Latino student success.
Association of American Colleges and Universities. Retrieved from
https://www.aacu.org/sites/default/files/files/assessinghips/GrowingKnowled
geNewsletter2014.pdf

Migliorini, L., Rania, N., & Cardinali, P. (2015). Intercultural learning context and
acculturation strategies. Procedia - Social and Behavioral Sciences, 171,
374-381. doi.org/10.1016/j.sbspro.2015.01.135

Morrison, D. (2014). How to make group work collaborative in online courses.
Four strategies. Online Learning
Insights.https://onlinelearninginsights.wordpress.com/tag/how-to-facilitate-
online-group-work/collaborative in online courses. Four strategies. Online
Learning Insights. https://onlinelearninginsights.wordpress.com/tag/how-to-
facilitate-online-group-work/

Mykota, D. B. (2015). A replication study on the multi-dimensionality of online
social presence. Turkish Online Journal of Educational Technology, 14(1),
11-18. Retrieved from www.tojet.net.

National Institute of Health. (2017). Cultural Respect. Clear Communication.
Retrieved from https://www.nih.gov/institutes-nih/nih-office-director/office-
communications-public-liaison/clear-communication/cultural-respect

Ojeda, L., Castillo, L. G., Meza, R. R., & Piña-Watson, B. (2014). Mexican
Americans in higher education: Cultural adaptation and marginalization as
predictors of college persistence intentions and life satisfaction. Journal of
Hispanic Higher Education, 13, 3-14. doi.org/10.1177/1538192713498899

Paletz, S. B. F., Miron-Spektor, E., & Lin, C. C. (2014). A cultural lens on
interpersonal conflict and creativity in multicultural environments.
Psychology of Aesthetics, Creativity, and the Arts, 8, 237-252.
doi:10.1037/a0035927

Plante, K., & Asselin, M. E. (2014). Best practices for creating social presence
and caring behaviors online. Nursing Education Perspectives, 35, 219-223.
doi:10.5480/13-1094.1

Plotts, C. (2018). Latino/a cultural perspectives of social presence: a case study.
International Journal of Educational Technology, 5(1), 29-36.

Posselt, J. & Lipson, K. S. (2016). Competition anxiety and depression in the
college classroom. Variations by student identity and fields of study. Journal
of College Student Development, 57(8) 973-989.
https://doi.org/10/1353/cds/2016.0094

Prause, D., & Mujtaba, B. (2015). Conflict management for diverse workplaces.
Journal of Business Studies Quarterly, 6(3), 13-22. Retrieved from
http://jbsq.org

Prilleltensky, I. (1999, June). Critical psychology and social justice. Concepts of
social justice in community psychology. Symposium at the Biennial Meeting
of the Society for Community Research and Action. New Haven CT.

Raes, E. Kyndt, E. Decuyper, S. Van den Bossche, P., & Dochy, F., (2015). An
exploratory study of group development and team learning. Human
Resource Development Quarterly, 26: 5-30. doi:10.1002/hrdq.21201

Rottman, A. & Rabidoux, S. (2017). How to provide meaningful feedback online.
Inside Higher Education. https://www.insidehighered.com/digital-

learning/views/2017/09/06/how-provide-meaningful-feedback-online-course

Safronova, L. B. (2014). The definition of social experience. A theoretical perspective. 18(2). Retrieved from https://zbirnyk.ipv.org.ua/en/archive/product/view/4/161Schutt, M., Allen, B.S. & Laumakis, M.A. (2009). The Effects of Instructor Immediacy Behaviors in Online-learning environments. *Quarterly Review of Distance Education, 10*(2), 135-148. Retrieved June 4, 2018 from https://www.learntechlib.org/p/103637/.

Schutt, M., Allen, B.S. & Laumakis, M.A. (2009). The Effects of instructor immediacy behaviors in online-learning environments. Quarterly Review of Distance Education, 10(2), 135-148. Retrieved June 4, 2018 from https://www.learntechlib.org/p/103637/.Sirin, S., & Ryce, P., Gupta, T., & Rogers-Sirin, L. (2013). The role of acculturative stress on mental health symptoms for immigrant adolescents: A longitudinal investigation. *Developmental Psychology, 49,* 736-748. doi.org/10.1037/a0028398

Sirin, S., & Ryce, P., Gupta, T., & Rogers-Sirin, L. (2013). The role of acculturative stress on mental health symptoms for immigrant adolescents: A longitudinal investigation.

Developmental Psychology, 49, 736-748. doi.org/10.1037/a0028398Snowball, J. D. (2014). Using interactive content and online activities to accommodate diversity in a large first year class. *Higher Education, 67,* 823-838. doi.org/10.1007/s10734-013- 9708-7

Soper, T., & Ukot, E. (2016). Social presence and cultural competence in the online-learning environment (OLE): A review of literature. *American Journal of Health Sciences, 7,* 9- 13. doi.org/10.19030/ajhs.v7i1.9692

Stebleton, M. J., Soria, K. M., & Huesman, R. L. (2014). First-generation students' sense of belonging, mental health, and use of counseling services at public research universities. *Journal of College Counseling, 17,* 6-17. doi:10.1002/j.2161-1882.2014.00044.x

Stevens, B. A., & Ellerbrock, L. S. (1995). Crisis intervention: An opportunity to change. ERIC Digest. Greensboro, NC: ERIC Clearinghouse on Counseling and Student Services.

Triandis, H. C. (1996). The psychological measurement of cultural syndromes. *American Psychologist, 51,* 407-415. doi:10.1037/0003-066X.51.4.407

Traindis, H.C. (1994). *Cultural and social behavior.* New York. McGraw Hill. Thompson, N. L., Miller, N. C., & Franz, D. P. (2013). Comparing online and face-to-face learning experiences for non-traditional students. *Quarterly Review of Distance Education, 14*(4), 233-251. Retrieved from http://www.infoagepub.com/quarterly-review- of-distance-education.html

Thompson, N. L., Miller, N. C., & Franz, D. P. (2013). Comparing online and face-to-face learning experiences for non-traditional students. Quarterly Review of Distance Education, 14(4), 233-251. Retrieved from http://www.infoagepub.com/quarterly-review- of-distance-education.html

Tuckman, B. W., & Jensen, M. A. C. (1977). Stages of small-group development revisited. Group & Organization Management, 2, 419-427. doi.org/10.1177/165960117700200404

Types of presence: Cognitive and social. University of California, Davis. Retrieved April 21, 2020 from https://canvas.ucdavis.edu/courses /34528/pages/types-of-presence-cognitive-and-social-presence

Van de Vijver, F. J. R., Blommaert, J., Gkoumasi, G., & Stogianni, M. (2015). On the need to broaden the concept of ethnic identity. *International Journal of Intercultural Relations, 46,* 36-46. doi:10.1016/j.ijintrel.2015.03.021

White, J. W., & Ali-Kahn, C. (2013). The role of academic discourse in minority students' academic assimilation. *American Secondary Education, 42*(1), 24-

43. Retrieved from https://www.ashland.edu/coe/about-college/american-secondary-education-journal

Zhao, H., Sullivan, K. P. H., & Mellenius, I. (2014). Participation, interaction and social presence: An exploratory study of collaboration in online peer review groups. *British Journal of Educational Technology, 45*, 807-819. doi.org/10.1111/bjet.12094

Zvolensky, M. J. (2016). Acculturative stress and experiential avoidance: relations, to depression, suicide, and anxiety symptoms among college students. *Cognitive Behaviour Therapy 45*(6) 501-517. https://doi.org/10.1080/16506073.2016.1205658

ABOUT THE AUTHOR

Dr. Courtney Plotts is a dynamic keynote speaker and presenter. Dr. Plotts has a Ph.D. in Psychology and at the time of this writing, is National Chair for the Council of At-Risk Student Education and Professional Standards. Dr. Plotts was recognized by the California Legislation in 2017 for a positive change in education. She consulted in the book, Small Teaching Online (Flower Darby and James Lang, 2019).

Dr. Plotts provides professional development sessions on best teaching and learning practices as well as counseling practices in face-to-face and online environments for first-generation, marginalized, and diverse populations. In 2020, she worked on the Space Between series of books focused on caring and connected behaviors in online spaces for African-American and LGBTQ+ students learning in virtual classrooms and spaces. These books are scheduled for publication 2020 and 2021. Dr. Plotts is also a practicing virtual school psychologist providing counseling and assessment service to students living in rural parts of Wyoming.

Dr. Plotts lives in Tampa, FL. She is married with two sons, two dogs, a cat, and enjoys reading and spending time with friends and family.

ABOUT THE BOOK

"I have not heard anyone address this topic in online spaces before" was a statement the author heard frequently when interviewed for education-based podcasts. This book equips faculty members with the knowledge and skills to enhance their curriculum selection, course design, discussions, and feedback in online and virtual spaces. If educators' practices and methodologies are not including consideration for student cultural attributes, the teachers and instructors are missing a 'real connection' – especially in virtual and online spaces.

This book is a 'must have' in teaching and learning practice. The author addresses questions that results in answers that targets a better understanding of how to increase the connecting with students in virtual educational spaces – specifically the LatinX culture and research-based and identified cultural way of learning. The idea of cultural adaptation to learning is critical to instructional effectiveness in online higher education environments.

This book provides clear foundations and examples of a specific viewpoint, background knowledge and skills, as well as small changes faculty can make in their content, discussions, and course development to better connect with and engage LatinX students in online spaces.

Made in the USA
Middletown, DE
18 September 2020